The Undiscovered

✳

The Undiscovered Country

Exploring
the Promise
of Death

✳

E K N A T H

E A S W A R A N

NILGIRI PRESS

First printing May 1996

The Blue Mountain Center of Meditation, founded in
Berkeley, California, in 1961 by Eknath Easwaran,
publishes books on how to lead the spiritual life
in the home and the community.
For information please write to
Nilgiri Press, Box 256, Tomales, California 94971

Printed on recycled, permanent paper.
The paper used in this publication meets the minimum
requirements of American National Standard for Information
Services - Permanence of Paper for Printed Library Materials,
ANSI Z39.48–1984

Library of Congress Cataloging in Publication Data:
Easwaran, Eknath.
The undiscovered country : exploring the promise of death /
Eknath Easwaran.
p. cm.
Includes bibliographical references and index.
ISBN 0–915132–84–2 (alk. paper). –
ISBN 0–915132–83–4 (pbk. : alk. paper)
1. Death–Religious aspects. 2. Spiritual life. I. Title.
BL504.E19 1996
291.2'3 – dc20   96–9968   CIP

Table of Contents

Introduction

In one of India's ancient epics there is an episode in which the hero learns a lesson about death. Five brothers, princes exiled from their rightful kingdom, are wandering in a forest and find themselves parched with thirst. The youngest goes for water and discovers an inviting lake with a white crane standing at its edge. He rushes forward, but before he can drink the crane speaks.

"Stop!" it cries. "This is my lake. If you touch this water without answering my questions, you will die."

Desperate, the young man ignores the warning. He bends to drink and falls dead by the water's edge.

In a few moments the next brother comes in search of the first. He too is tormented by thirst, and he bends down at the lake's edge to drink.

Just as he is about to slake his thirst, the crane speaks to him: "Stop! If you touch this water without answering my questions, you will die." But even though the young prince sees his brother lying dead nearby, he is so driven by thirst that he cannot help himself. He too falls dead at the side of his brother.

One by one, two more brothers meet the same fate. Only the eldest, grieving where his brothers lie, agrees to set aside his anguish and his burning thirst and to submit to the crane's sphinxlike riddles. One of these is particularly poignant: "What is the most surprising thing in life?"

The prince replies, "That although a man may see people dying every day, he never thinks that he will die."

Finally, the crane reveals himself to be none other than the God of Truth in disguise, and he restores the dead brothers to life.

This story has haunted me since I was a child in India. It touches something very deep in our predicament as human beings: partly physical, partly spiritual, trying to understand the world into which we have been born. We are not wholly at home in this world of change and death. The soul is in exile here, a wanderer, a stranger in a strange land, traveling inexorably toward what Shakespeare called "the undiscovered country" that is death. And we long for something more. Life itself – and the fact of death – compels us to press certain crucial questions: "Where have I come from? What will happen to me when I die? Is there no way I can go beyond death?"

These questions are the beginning of wisdom. The confrontation with death brings a sense of urgency about discovering the purpose of life – and not only of our life, but of the lives of all those we love. For death is very near, waiting for each one of us. It is because we do not remember this that most of our attention goes to goals and possessions and activities that have little lasting value.

Nothing in life is more important than the fact of death, and nothing more urgent than learning to overcome it – not in an afterlife, but here and now. In the scriptures of almost all religions – Christian, Jewish, Muslim, Buddhist, Hindu – the promise of eternal life is given.

People usually understand this only as an inspiring metaphor, not to be taken with the same gravity as scientific truth. But the mystics say that it is time that is an illusion; eternity is the reality. At our birth, a kind of shadow falls over our consciousness, hiding everything but this brief span we call our mortal life. Only the mystics see beyond this veil of shadows to the eternal light shining beyond.

When I was a boy in India, growing up in a large ancestral family, death would come not infrequently to those near and dear to me. Whenever a death took place, my grandmother, who was my spiritual teacher, would always insist that I accompany her to the scene of sorrow, even when I was still an impressionable and sensitive child. I remember looking at the dead body in utter disbelief. I just could not believe that the person was dead, and I was too young to understand any explanation. As I sat by the side of dying people while my grandmother held their hand, it used to torture me. Even in my dreams, I long remembered the sight of this agony I witnessed during the days when I was growing up at my grandmother's feet.

Later on, when through her blessing I began to turn inwards and practice meditation, I realized why she had taken me to those scenes of bereavement. It was to make me ask if there is any way to transcend death. Her inspiration enabled me to understand that in the midst of life I am in death, and to want above everything else to go beyond death in this very life.

In the life of every spiritually aware person, the time comes when he or she questions whether death is inevitable. This is not an intellectual question at all, but an experience in which some lurking suspicion comes into our consciousness that whispers that we are not mortal. Once we hear this, there is great hope, and a great desire to turn our back upon lesser desires so that we can devote ourselves to making the supreme discovery that we are eternal.

There is a common misunderstanding that complete Self-realization – or "union with God," or "entering into the kingdom of heaven" – comes only after the death of the body. But a medieval Indian mystic, Kabir, who was claimed by both Hindus and Muslims, tells us that if we attain spiritual awareness now, in this life, we attain it forever. If we don't attain it now, it will not happen after death simply because the body has been left behind. Kabir says, "What you call salvation belongs to the time before death."

This is the universal message of mysticism all over the world: complete understanding of our eternal, spiritual nature can be realized while we are here on earth, in this life. "What is found now is found then," Kabir says. "If you find nothing now, you will simply end up with an apartment in the city of death."

According to all spiritual teachers, this life is only one small chapter in the book of eternity. When the body comes to an end, it is resolved into its constituents. But the resident, the Self, is not going to die. When the body dies, that is not the end of the story. We needn't believe in reincarnation to understand this. Whether we believe in one life or many, we can learn to live this life in love and wisdom. And when we live today rightly, tomorrow has got to be right.

The important thing is that we wake ourselves up from this dream of self-centered, separate existence we call living. As long as we dream on, so long will we be exiles in the realms of death, helplessly pitted against an opponent we can never vanquish.

In another story in our epics, the same wise prince who answered the riddle of the crane is tricked into a dice game. It is a heartbreaking episode in which the noble prince, pitted against a cheat, first loses his gold, then his jewels, then his lands, and finally his brothers and even himself – all gambled away in a game that is rigged. When I see this painful episode portrayed in the Indian ballet, it reminds me that we are all playing with dice. Every one of us is in a grand casino where we gamble against death every day. Death and his allies are seated on one side of the table; we are seated on the other. And every time we throw the dice, Death says to the croupier, "Collect! They have lost." But instead of losing a golden crown or a kingdom, we lose, gradually, our vitality, our strength, and finally life itself. "Give me your sight," Death says, and as the years advance, we give it. Then Death says, "Give me your hearing." And he is prepared to wait. Sooner or later Death will take everything, either little by little or all at once.

I appreciate many of the advances of modern medicine, and I know that science and technology have done a great deal to put off the ravages of time; but I never forget that death is waiting, and raising the stakes day by day. According to the theory of reincarnation, we have led many, many lives, and we have lost time and time again. In every life, Death shouts his victory: "He has lost! She has lost! I have won!"

It may look as if we cannot possibly win, yet we were born to conquer decay and death. This is the living message of all spiritual teachers, as urgent today as it was in times past. To vanquish death we have only to discover who we really are: not the perishable, material body but the eternal Self, which dwells in the body but does not die when the body dies.

A Small Incident

Our birth is but a sleep and a forgetting:
The Soul that rises with us, our life's Star,
Hath had elsewhere its setting,
And cometh from afar:
Not in entire forgetfulness,
And not in utter nakedness,
But trailing clouds of glory do we come
From God, who is our home. . . .

—William Wordsworth,
"Intimations of Immortality"

A few years ago a friendly stray cat showed up at our place, and he quickly wove himself into the fabric of our lives. My friend Mary, who has a weakness for cats, called him Charles, and he soon learned that if he showed up at certain times of the morning and evening, he would get a little dish of bread with milk and a place of his own in the hierarchy of dogs and cats that roam the neighborhood.

Charles's need for affection went very deep. Every evening as I went out for a walk, he used to come out of nowhere to rub his body against my legs as if trying to trip me up. And when my walk was over he would lurk in the shadows, crossing and recrossing the path while I gave the dogs their goodnight snack. Then, once the dogs were gone and he was sure no one would chase him away, he would come to the door to get his treat too. I used to stroke him while he gobbled his tidbit and purred like a little sewing machine.

Then one day he did not come. I waited awhile, then left his snack on the back porch. In the morning I found some birds pecking at it, but Charles never came. Nor did he come that evening. The next morning Mary told me that Charles was no more.

Now there is no one to trip me up on the sidewalk as I walk home in the dark. And I miss him – miss his nightly panhandling, his responsive purr, all the little impediments he placed in my path each evening. Such a small incident, we might say. Just a footnote to a busy day. But in a profound sense it was a deeply significant event.

One night Charles was rubbing against my legs, eating at my feet, purring under my hand. The next day he was gone. He was here on earth for ten years or so; has he now disappeared? When someone dies, has that person simply vanished? Someone whom yesterday we loved and cherished, who today has faded away like last night's dream?

In village India, it is impossible to be ignorant of death. Lives are too interconnected. Everyone knows everyone else, and it is not uncommon to hear that someone you saw only the other day, or with whom you went to school, or whose mango tree you used to climb, has passed from this life completely. It is a continual reminder of the transiency of all life. There is no isolation from the dramas of birth and death as there often is in this country; life ebbs out in the presence of family and friends, and the grief of the family adds to the agony of the dying. But whether in India or America or any other land, in the presence of death the sensitive person can't help asking, Where has this favorite uncle gone? Just last Christmas he was visiting with us. That girl I knew in college, whose smile was so radiant and whose laugh was so free – is she no more? Or has she, as one mystic puts it, simply stepped into another room? If they have not just vanished, where have they gone?

If I had to explain what has happened, I would say, "They are dead, yet they are not dead." The intellect may turn away in confusion from such statements and say, "Impossible!" But it is not impossible. To myself I do not use a phrase like "she is dead." She has shed her body; but she was not that body. The body was her house; she was the resident, the Self.

✳

In the Hindu and Buddhist scriptures, all this is placed against a breathtakingly vast backdrop. When mystics from these traditions speak of an individual "person," they do not mean someone who lives for just a few decades. The Sanskrit term *jiva* refers to the individual soul as it evolves through many, many lives. You and I, they would say, have been evolving from the time the earth was born, billions of years ago. This is entirely compatible with biological evolution. It simply asserts that biology is not the whole story: that connecting successive individual lives, as creatures evolve, there is a vital lifeline of consciousness that is not terminated by death.

This question is not confined to the Eastern mystics only. Saint Augustine, in the beginning of his *Confessions,* pleads, "O tell me, Lord, whether my infancy but followed upon some other stage of my life that had died, or was that all, which I experienced in my mother's womb? What was before then, my sweet Lord? Was I anywhere or anyone?"

It is not necessary to accept reincarnation to live a life of wisdom. In fact, it can be a distraction to become concerned with investigations into past lives. In India, where everyone takes reincarnation for granted, we never talk about it, never speculate about it. But for anyone with an open mind, the theory of reincarnation offers some sound explanations that cannot easily be dismissed.

Against the backdrop of reincarnation, we

have been shaping ourselves life after life through our personal pattern of living. As human beings, we have the capacity to choose: to live violently or nonviolently, to live selfishly or selflessly, to live in such a way that our spiritual awareness grows or to hinder our own fulfillment. Once we enter the human context, the Buddha says, everything is in our hands. No fate compels us; no outside power can take from us the responsibility for wise choices which is our human heritage.

In this perspective, each of us is continuously evolving. Just as we pass through the stages of life from birth to death, at the end of one life we pass on to another. If we find this difficult to understand, it is largely because our idea of who we are is so riveted to the physical level, the biological organism. We cannot remember any existence at all before the birth of the body. "I just can't remember ever being anyone but Fred Smith," we might say. But the Buddha would not find this kind of evidence compelling. He would ask, "Do you remember what you were like when you were six months old? No teeth, no way to talk or walk about, and your idea of happiness was chewing the ears of your teddy bear. Now you have all sorts of teeth, and the only bears you are interested in are those that compete with the bulls on Wall Street. Everything is different. What makes you say you are the same person?" Yet we are – even though everything about us has changed and we can no longer remember those earliest years.

On the physical level, of course, death seems to be a much more sudden and final change than aging. But as far as our thoughts, desires, aspirations, and values are concerned, the same personality continues after the physical body falls away. Once we rise above a strictly physical perspective, we see the thread of continuity through all these changes.

The Bhagavad Gita, the treasured Indian scriptural classic, says:

> As the same person inhabits a body through childhood, youth, and age, so at the time of death he or she attains another body. The wise are not deluded by these changes.

Just as you and I were once babies, grew into children, went to school, perhaps went on to college – each year a little different, yet each year still the same person – so through the inexorable passage of time we enter old age. Finally, like a snake sloughing off its skin, the Self within us sheds the old body in the hour of death and prepares to take on a new one.

I can illustrate this on the level of everyday experience. Just as Charles left us recently, so – in a different sense – did the son of a dear friend of ours. Christo is in the air now, on his way to Greece with his mother and grandmother. We will miss him, but at the same time we know that after fifteen days he will be back. We believe this because we believe in geography. After all, the only thing we really know is that Christo and his mother are gone. But we believe that there is a country called Greece, even if we have never been there. We believe there is a village called Milochori, even if scarcely anyone has been there. We believe that a jet plane can bring these people back. We believe in geography, we believe in jets, but we find it hard to believe in the words of the Buddha. Shakespeare, too, said that death is a kind of place: "The undiscovered country from whose bourne / No traveler returns" – at least, not with the same name and form. The jiva does return: "not the same person," the Buddha explains, "but not someone different either."

Again, look at Christo. His mother will come back very much the same as when she left, in a tearing hurry to attend to all the correspondence that has piled up on her desk while she was gone. But Christo will have changed a little. Five is an impressionable age. He will have picked up a few Greek words, like "Eureka!" He will probably have new clothes and a new way of walking, and when I ask him who he is today, he will not be a fireman or a cowboy; he'll be a *princeps*. But we will not be fooled. We will know that he is still Christo.

Similarly, in the next life the jiva is a little different yet still the same. There is a continuity in the deeply ingrained ways of thinking and feeling and acting which we have developed over many lives. These deep habits are what Indian psychology calls *samskaras*, and they shape our actions, our behavior, our very destiny in life after life because those which we are not able to work out in one life carry on to be worked out in the next. Understanding this continuity of samskaras brings tremendous motivation to live wisely. You know that everything you do is shaping your personal character and prospects, not only tomorrow but in the life to come.

Read any great spiritual teacher, East or West. Behind every line will be their personal testimony that preparing for the inevitable journey into our next existence is the most relevant issue in life. Making money, for example, is not good or bad; it is irrelevant. As you say in this country, you can't take it with you. If you could take it with you, it might make sense to hoard as much as you can. Similarly, if you could hoard pleasures and put them in a safe deposit box which you could open in the hereafter, I would say, "Sure, devote your life to pleasure." But unfortunately, none of this is going to cross the border with us. In fact, very little of it gets to the border at all. We can't even carry pleasure over to the next day.

Imagine us packing our boxes, hoarding, planning what we'll carry with us on our forty-pound allotment and what we'll send ahead. "Man," the Buddha would say, "you can't take any of this! Work on what you *can* take with you" – in fact, on what you can't help taking with you. Every thought we are going to take with us, every word, every deed, every desire. Those which do not bear fruit in this life will bear fruit in the next, as they go on shaping our destiny.

With every thought, the Buddha would say, we are working on our destiny. When a sculptor creates an elephant, each touch of the chisel shapes the stone. While carving an eye the artist barely strokes the surface, but those delicate touches are as vital as the rough shaping blows. There is no such thing as an unimportant blow. Similarly, every thought shapes our lives. There is no such thing as a little thought, no such thing as an unimportant thought. It may be heavy, it may be light, but it always should be well directed.

Therefore, the Buddha says, we should not blame others for our lot. We always have a choice in what we think, and as we think, so we live. If our thoughts are selfish, we will live in a world shaped by selfish thoughts – not a very pleasant world to live in. But if our thoughts are selfless, we will gradually enter the kingdom of heaven right here on earth. We will feel deeply secure, we will be loved and respected, and most important, we will have won our own self-respect, for we will know that our life is a fountain from which those around us can quench their thirst.

When we see how much violence there is on this earth, how much injustice and sorrow, every one of us must be tempted to ask why. The Buddha would reply compassionately, "You see only one brief flash that you call life. There is much more to life than that. If you could see the whole vast saga of evolution, all the things done, said, and thought in the past that come to bear on the present life, you would see an almost infinite web of cause and effect." This attitude is not fatalistic. Rather, it allows us to assume responsibility for our own lives.

Aldous Huxley, well before he became interested in reincarnation, ascribed personality to chance in a short poem:

A million million spermatozoa,
     All of them alive:
Out of their cataclysm but one poor Noah

Dare hope to survive.
And among that billion minus one
  Might have chanced to be
Shakespeare, another Newton, a new Donne –
  But the One was Me.

Huxley makes this observation in great surprise. I would say, "Aldous, it *had* to be you." To me it's so obvious. Each of us had to be who we are.

This is not an intellectual conclusion; it is an experiential realization. When it comes, you accept yourself completely. After all, no one else has made you the way you are.

When you understand this on a deep level, it lifts an immense burden. There is great joy in this understanding: no jealousy, no envy, no self-pity, no "why wasn't it otherwise?" or "if only I could have been . . ." Everything is just right for you to deal with your problems, contribute to the rest of life, and grow. Toward the end of his life, Swami Vivekananda, a distinguished spiritual teacher from Bengal, wrote to a close disciple: "I am glad I was born, glad I suffered so, glad I did make big blunders, glad to enter peace." Everything falls into a complete pattern; even your mistakes, when you look back, are seen to be part of growth.

✳

Physical evolution can be explained in physical terms, but to account for the evolution of individual consciousness we need to speak in terms of energy. For this purpose we can describe personality, the jiva, as a field of forces, not unlike the field around a magnet: forces which not only shape our lives but affect the thoughts and actions of those around us. Much more than our bodies, this field of forces is really who we are as limited, separate creatures.

In a sense, this field of forces is a packet of the primal energy called *prana* in Sanskrit. According to the Upanishads, probably the oldest mystical documents in any religion, all the forces of the phenomenal world – gravitation, electromagnetism, and the rest – are forms of prana. When the sun shines, it is prana that shines. When the eagle flies, it is prana that flies. When the heart beats, when neurons fire, when food is digested and remade into the constituents of our bodies, all this is prana – for prana is the energy of life.

This energy is not merely physical. When we think, feel, desire, will, or love, we draw on prana – the same prana that empowers the physiological processes that make for health or illness. And when prana leaves, the body dies. The body, after all, is only a carton. Prana is its contents.

Wherever prana goes, the Upanishads say, the mind and the senses follow obediently, tugging at their caps and saying, "Yes, sir. Whatever you say, sir. Wherever you go, sir." Without prana the brain and the sense organs may be physiologically intact, but they cannot function.

The Upanishads dramatize this with a homely story. One day the senses got puffed up. Each believed it was the most important. "I'm going to do my own thing," Sight announced. "Why should I hang around with dull fellows like Touch here?" Hearing said, "Me, too. I don't need anybody to tell me what to do."

Taste, Touch, and Smell agreed, and so each decided to go off on its own.

Finally Prana got tired of the bickering. "Now it's my turn," he announced. "Goodbye!" He got up to leave, wrenching vitality from the body the way a tethered wild stallion tears its stakes out of the ground. "Stop!" all the senses pleaded. "Don't leave us. You're our real chief, Prana; we're all dead without you."

Prana is never extinguished. It *is* parted from its physical container, the body, at the time of death, but this is not the end of the journey. For those who do not identify themselves with the body, consciousness is not ruptured at the time of death. Such a person simply sheds the body like an old jacket which is worn out. No one's consciousness is ruptured when he takes off his shirt at night. Similarly, at the time of death, the great mystics testify that the body falls away with no break in consciousness because their awareness is no longer individual; it has become universal. No longer confined to the personal, it has expanded to include all of life.

All of us have moments when we forget ourselves in helping others. In these moments, we step out of ourselves: we really cease, if only for an instant, to be a separate person. Those are moments of immortality, right on earth.

I think Lord Tennyson in a poetic reverie is said to have had a passing glimpse of himself going into boundless being. Just for a moment, he felt he was no longer subject to the conditioning of a private person but had an insight into the unitive state. It was a fleeting, poetic experience. But in the case of the great mystics, this is a permanent realization.

Saint John of the Cross has captured this mystical experience in poetry that is unequaled in its beauty and its depth of experience. Saint John *knew* he was not the body because in a mystical rapture that he called the "dark night" of union with God he had left his body, his house, behind:

> In a dark night,
> Inflamed with love's impatient longing
> – Oh, what good fortune! –
> I went out unseen,
> My house being now all silent;
> . . .
> I lost and forgot myself,

My face resting on my Beloved;
All things ceased, and I surrendered myself,
Leaving my cares
Forgotten among the lilies.

Mystics like Saint John of the Cross <u>know</u> through personal experience that they <u>are one</u> <u>with the whole</u>, in which <u>there</u> is <u>neither birth</u> <u>nor death</u>.

✳

Spiritual teachers from all religions tell us that the <u>unity of</u> life is a <u>timeless</u> truth which we cannot ignore without harm. But today this truth is largely forgotten. Over a long, long period of preoccupation with private pursuits, basking in our separateness from others, we have not only denied the unity of life but completely forgotten it.

Imagine a young man – I'll call him Sam – who lives in a geodesic dome, an apt symbol of the earth. When Sam enters his dome, he leaves the world behind him: its trees, its flowers, its clouds, its cars, all the people outside. Everything he wants is in his dome. After all, he has attractive furnishings: a nice Turkish carpet, Danish furniture, a collection of houseplants, conveniences like a microwave oven and a popcorn maker, a state-of-the-art sound system and a VCR. If he stays there long enough, he begins to forget everything and everybody outside. The external world, the wider universe in which the dome is only a planet, becomes unreal to him. After some years, if you ask him questions about the rest of the world, he will say, "I don't remember." Eventually he will say, "I doubt whether there is an external world of which this dome is a part." And finally he will say, "The outside world does not exist. Nothing exists but this dome."

When we live for ourselves and confine our attention to narrow, personal concerns – making money, going on an exciting vacation, getting our picture on the cover of a popular magazine – we are a fragment in a world of fragments. Gradually we find that it is difficult for a fragment to find a place in the world and give a good account of itself. A fragment can only be a wanderer in life, buffeted by the winds of pleasure and pain, whirled round and round in the storms of birth and death. But if we can break through the private little personality, the jiva, and realize our real Self, we become a significant, beneficial influence in life. We are magnified until not only our family but our community and our whole society benefits from our lives. We have only to look at the lives of such men and women of God as Saint Francis, Saint Teresa of Avila, Sri Ramakrishna, and, in our own century, Mahatma Gandhi to see that this is so.

Such mystics see the presence of God everywhere: in the sky, in the sun and moon, in animals and birds, and of course in the "human face divine." For the God-conscious person, the wind sighing in the trees whispers of God; the waves sweeping across the beach sing the name of God. Everything is pervaded by the presence of God. When the mind is permeated like this with the consciousness of God, we know that we are the Self, a spark of the divine. We come into eternal life, and at the time of death, as Sri Ramakrishna said, we simply step from one room to another.

✳

> I am Time, the destroyer of all;
> I have come to consume the world.

These are words that made the Bhagavad Gita known the world over. It was this verse that came to Robert Oppenheimer's mind as he watched the first atomic bomb explode across the desert sky. The devastating Sanskrit word used here is *kala,* which has a double-edged meaning: "time" and "death." Time *is* death; time is separateness. Its all-devouring jaws are following us always, closer than our shadow.

As we grow older and our family and friends begin to pass away, we see how relentlessly time is pursuing all of us; every death should remind us of the imminence of our own. People with whom we played and laughed – they are no more. Great figures who have walked across the stage of life – they are no more. Dynasties and empires have returned to dust. It is only because of the mercy of God that you and I survive each day. Those who are sensitive to this have tremendous motivation to take to the spiritual path and slay the monster of time and death.

The Buddha tells us, "Our life of separateness may be compared to a dream, a phantasm, a bubble, a shadow, a drop of dew, a flash of lightning." It is good to bear in mind how evanescent life is so that we do not get caught up in living just for ourselves, postponing the voyage across the sea of separate existence that is called *samsara* in Sanskrit, the cycle of birth and death.

For a long time I took it for granted that immortality was a figure of speech. It was by observing my grandmother's attitude toward death that I began slowly to understand that immortality is an actual quest, a living search that all people with drive and enthusiasm can undertake in this very life, beginning this very day. When I was a little boy I would sometimes say, "Granny, when I die . . ." But she would never let me say more. Clapping her hand over my mouth, she would assure me firmly: "You will never die."

Jackets

> *An eternal part of me enters into the world,*
> *assuming the powers of action and perception*
> *and a mind immersed in the material realm.*
> *When the divine Self enters and leaves a body,*
> *it takes these along as the wind carries a scent*
> *from place to place. . . . The deluded do not see*
> *the Self when it leaves the body or when it*
> *dwells within it. They do not see the Self*
> *enjoying the world or acting in it. But those*
> *who have the eye of wisdom see.*
> — *Sri Krishna in the Bhagavad Gita*

Many years ago, when I came to this country on
the Fulbright exchange program, I was asked by
the authorities where in the United States I
would like to go. "I'll be at home anywhere," I
assured them. "But please remember that I
come from South India. I'm not used to cold.
Until I was sixteen, not only had I never seen

snow, I had never seen anyone who had seen snow." The State Department, with its peculiar sense of humor, promptly sent me to the University of Minnesota.

I arrived in summer, so I thought I had come to the right place. But then winter came, not with a whimper but with a bang, and it found me completely unprepared. Below-zero temperature had not meant anything to me before. I was appalled to see the thermometer drop to minus ten without any sign of stopping. My friends from Minnesota laughed. "Just wait," they warned. "Winter hasn't even begun."

Then another foreign exchange professor returned from reconnaissance with good news. "There are tunnels connecting our dorms with the cafeteria!" he said. After that he did not emerge. He lived like a troglodyte, or a man in a submarine.

But I decided I would go on having my walks, snow or no snow. I put on clothes until I looked like an abominable snowman. My overcoat alone was so heavy that it hung from its peg on a chain. If I wanted exercise, all I had to do was lift that coat down and put it on. I felt like Sir

Gawain, ready to be hoisted onto his horse with a crane.

Underneath that coat I wore a sweater. Beneath that was a flannel shirt; beneath the shirt, a T-shirt. And of course underneath everything was the brown jacket made in India that I call my body.

By the time I put all this on and went outside, nobody could recognize me. They couldn't even see me; all they could see was this mammoth overcoat. If somebody spoke to me on the street, I felt he was really speaking to my mammoth. "How are you today? Did you sleep well?" I wanted to say, "No, thank you. I was hung up all night long"

The profound German mystic Meister Eckhart talks of the coverings that hide the soul: "A human being has so many skins inside, covering the depths of the heart. We know so many things, but we don't know ourselves! Why, thirty or forty skins or hides, as thick and hard as an ox's or a bear's, cover the soul. Go into your own ground and learn to know yourself there."

I was a walking example of what Meister Eckhart says. But where I was wearing rather prosaic wool and flannel and jersey and cotton, the jackets the mystics talk about are all beautifully tailored, custom made. Here there is no mass buying from Macy's basement. Each layer is made to fit me perfectly, and me alone.

Eckhart's is a wonderful, clear image of "thirty or forty skins" covering the soul. Hindu scriptures use a similar image, simplified into what are called the "five sheaths" or jackets. It is these five sheaths that have to be taken off, one after another, if we are to realize who we really are and understand how the jiva lives on after the last great change called death.

*

The outermost jacket, the overcoat, is the body. Just as a coat is made of tweed or camel hair, in Sanskrit the body is "the jacket made of food."

A few years ago an enterprising concern in the Bay Area offered to freeze your body for a handsome sum and keep it in an icebox in a state of suspended animation for a hundred years so that you could wake up into a "brave new world." This seems to be the limit we can reach in our idea of immortality: making the body last longer. I am not against making the body last longer when it is serving some useful purpose, but immortality has nothing to do with biological longevity. After all, this firm is only freezing the jacket, not the person. If you think of immortality in terms of long-lived garments, it is only natural to come up with some rather unsatisfying ways of attaining it.

The body is part of the phenomenal world, limited in time just as it is in space. As long as we identify with the body, therefore, we are subject to these same limitations. But if we can cut through our obsessive identification with the body and the other sheaths, death is no more a rupture in consciousness than is taking off a coat.

Within limits, identification with the body varies from person to person and from time to time. Even without reference to the spiritual life, there have been exceptional artists whose body-consciousness was much less than that of most other human beings because of their immense concentration. Ravi Shankar and Yehudi Menuhin, when they are performing, are probably not aware of the body at all. Great scientists, too, often show this capacity. When Albert Einstein sat down at his desk in the morning, he was so absorbed in his line of reasoning that often he would not move for hours on end, not even to take notes. In the afternoon he went to his desk again to set to paper the results of his morning's inquiry.

At such times there is scarcely any connection with the physical jacket. I once heard a story about a brilliant young physics student at the University of Göttingen in the days when physics was flourishing at the dawn of relativity and quantum theory. He became so rapt in the formulae he was working out in his head that he fell down in the street and just lay there. A distressed bystander rushed over and tried to help him to his feet. "Leave me alone!" the young man cried. "Can't you see I'm thinking?"

This capacity for absorption is not confined to distinguished artists and thinkers. Go to a casino and watch a compulsive gambler: when the roulette wheel is spinning, all his concentration is right there on the wheel. You can take the wallet out of his hip pocket and he won't even feel it go. All these are clues to an important truth: as concentration deepens, our compulsive identification with the body weakens. For a short while, we slip out of the coat of the body and identify ourselves with what is underneath.

✳

Beneath the overcoat of the body is a garment called "the sheath made of prana," vital energy, as finely tailored as an Italian sports jacket. This is a much finer, more subtle "body" than the physical body. We cannot, of course, see this sheath with our physical eyes, but we can sense its presence. Don't we often talk of "energy levels" and make remarks like "Cynthia just doesn't have much energy today"? When we do, we are making comments about the vital sheath, which plays an essential role in health. Without vitality, though our physical organs may be intact, they are as lifeless as a coat without a wearer.

Vital energy or prana is closely connected with the senses: the activities of seeing, hearing, touching, tasting, and smelling. It is through the senses that vitality is used and, sometimes, abused. Whenever the senses are overstimulated, we are tied more and more tightly into this second jacket, while at the same time wearing it out at an accelerated rate. Conversely, when we do not indulge the senses, we wear this jacket loosely, comfortably, like an elegant Armani creation, and it continues to be strong and beautiful for many years.

In the case of the mystics, whose senses are completely trained, this sheath can be taken off. When they are absorbed in meditation, consciousness is temporarily free from the distractions of the outer world and turned completely within. For the senses are the ties that keep consciousness linked to the outer world of change. In the stillness of the senses, we are much, much closer to the timeless, deathless world of which the scriptures of all religions speak. But three more jackets still need to be removed to uncover our real Self.

✳

Beneath my overcoat and sports jacket is the next covering: the sweater "made out of mind." This is a custom-made sweater, with all kinds of strange and wonderful designs knit into it. And it is very difficult to take off, because it has no buttons. You just don't know where to start.

Once I was given a hand-knit turtleneck sweater for Christmas. I wasn't accustomed to turtlenecks, but this was a beautiful sweater made especially for me by a close friend, so I wanted to wear it right away. Some way or other I got it on, but I couldn't get it off. I felt like a turtle trapped inside its shell.

That is how it is with the mind. When you get angry, how many times have you said to yourself, "I wish I could get out of this mood!" You are miserable, you are making everybody else miserable, but you just can't change your mind. There you are with the sweater halfway on and halfway off, and you can't breathe, you can't see; even your cries for help are muffled.

But amazing as it may sound, it is possible to slip out of the constricting turtleneck of the mind. Only then will we be able to see life clearly and breathe freely. In fact, only then will we be able to move in complete freedom – using our hands to come to the aid of others, using our arms to reach out to embrace others.

*

The fourth garment, called in Sanskrit the shirt "made of the intellect," usually consists of synthetic fabric. Or, to be charitable, it is a blend: mostly synthetic with some natural fibers here and there.

In other words, the intellectual sheath is mostly made up of other people's opinions: what we have read in books, heard on TV, picked up from the papers or from "news and opinion" magazines. I believe it was Robert Louis Stevenson who said that most of us, if we had to wait ten minutes for a train, wouldn't have two notions to rub together. An original, genuine idea is rare.

Yet the intellectual sheath is a valuable, precious garment. When the intellect is strong and sound, there is a certain "rage to know" that is a very healthy sign in any person. The intellect can ask important questions about life and death, why we are here and where we might be going. The difficulty arises because the intellect can ask these questions but not answer them. With its inherent limitations, the intellect – subtle and profound as it is – cannot go beyond the boundary of subject and object, cannot understand the underlying unity of life, and therefore cannot understand what has existed before this life and what may exist after it. The intellect can discern information but is helpless to gain wisdom.

It is the confusion of information and wisdom that ties us up in the intellectual sheath. Most of us in the modern world believe that by gathering more and more information about the world outside us, we will eventually come to know life's inmost secrets. That is why we follow with such avid curiosity probes into the bowels of the earth, flights into the outer reaches of the universe, and the monitoring of a fetus in the mother's womb. These are fascinating ventures, but they are never going to satisfy our need to understand the fundamental mysteries which haunt sensitive people everywhere: Who are we? For what purpose have we come into this life? These questions may at first glance seem simple, yet we are born, grow up, get married, raise a family, buy and sell, grow old, and die without ever knowing who we are.

To know who we are, we have to take off the intellectual sheath and leap beyond the duality of subject and object. When we have accomplished this extraordinary performance, there is only one garment left – the most difficult of all to remove.

*

Beneath the intellect is "the garment of the ego." The ego is the final covering, and it clings to us so closely and is so elusive that it is like the sheerest of undergarments woven of gossamer silk. In India, which has been noted for its master weavers since ancient times, there is a kind of silk that is so thin and so fine that you can draw yards and yards of it through a tiny finger ring.

The fabric of the ego is like that – but, paradoxically, it is also tough and unyielding.

The word Eckhart uses, "skin," is particularly appropriate here, because we are not merely dressed in the ego; we are trapped in it. We simply cannot shed this innermost garment by ourselves.

This morning I was talking with a friend when her little boy ran up flailing his arms and wailing. "Mommy!" he cried. "Help me! I can't get this off." His little fingers couldn't manage the buttons of his parka. She undid them and pulled the parka over his arms.

The wonderful Bengali mystic Sri Ramakrishna says this is just what the Divine Mother does for us. By no amount of our own effort can the last sheath of separateness be thrown away. It is we who are exerting the effort; how can we remove ourselves? It's like lifting yourself with your own bootstraps. In every religion, great mystics have testified that they eventually reached a point on the spiritual path where they could go no further on their own. Then all they could do was call, "Mother! I've done all I can, but I'm still caught. Please get me free!"

In simple language, this is what orthodox mystics call the miracle of divine grace. The Katha Upanishad says:

> The supreme Self cannot be known through study of the scriptures, nor through the intellect, nor through hearing discourses about it. It can be known only by those whom the Self chooses. Verily unto them does the Self reveal itself!

For those who pursue the spiritual life with sustained enthusiasm, taking off jacket after jacket, the great day comes when an irresistible divine force, present in the depths of our consciousness, unbuttons this last jacket of separateness from inside. It falls away, and in an instant we see ourselves as we really are: all love, all wisdom, the same in every creature on earth. Death can no longer hold any terrors for us, for we know without a doubt that we are the immortal, immutable Self – that we were never born and can never die.

✳

It is not too difficult to understand that the body is a house we live in, a car we drive, a garment we wear. In my talks, when I say, "You are not the body," I usually get appreciative nods from the audience. But when I say, "And you are not the mind, either," people begin to protest, "Now, wait a minute!"

The mind is an endlessly fascinating subject, and the world of the mind is as vast as the world we experience outside. It is no exaggeration to say that crossing the world of the mind is just as adventurous as crossing the Pacific on a raft or journeying to the moon.

It is through the practice of meditation that we can best get to know the world of the mind and transcend it – and, along with it, the world ruled by the laws of change and death. Unlike concentration on external phenomena, meditation is essentially a discipline for deepening concentration within so that one by one we cease to identify with the jackets hiding the Self.

But meditation by itself is not enough to

break the physical and mental bonds that keep us from going inwards. Along with meditation, we have to withdraw our attention little by little from the innumerable desires – for pleasure, profit, power, prestige – which tie us to the body and mind. Meditation on the one hand, and our vigilance during the rest of day on the other, together gradually free us from the compulsive desires that hold us captive in the kingdom of change and death. The mind is essentially a series of desires. To desire, to desire, to desire – that is the nature of the mind.

Let me say at the outset that it is necessary to distinguish between two kinds of desire. The first are compulsive desires; the others, likely to be fewer in number, are right desires. In the first, I am trying to get things for myself, trying to grab, to possess, to manipulate, under the compulsion of craving. The more we yield to this first kind of desire, the more we will be bound to the body and mind. Unless we can say no to such desires, our responses are not free. But not all desires are selfish and compulsive. Among right desires, the noblest is selfless love. When we want to help someone even if he or she has been unkind, that is selfless love. When we want to foster our spiritual growth or make a contribution to our family or community, that is right desire. In right desires we are not bound by stimulus and response; we are free to respond as we choose.

When we can look with detachment, it becomes clear that most of our desires have nothing to do with our approval. They crowd into the mind like fans rushing into a soccer stadium or first-nighters at a new movie – about half a dozen at a time, each hanging on to the coattails of the next. "Why bother with a ticket?" they say. "This fellow must be asleep; there's nobody at the door. Let's just go in; he won't even know."

How long could a movie theater operate on this basis? The theaters I know of have all kinds of checkpoints. You have to stand in a queue and get your ticket; then you file past some fellow who tears the ticket in two and says, "Enjoy the show." Yet in the movie theater of the mind, desires do not have to queue up or buy a ticket. They barge in and sit wherever they like. There is no one to stop them at the door. In fact, there is no door; there are not even any walls. Desires just do what they like, and whichever is biggest gets the best seat. A fat, selfish desire can occupy a whole box; a little desire has to sit on the floor in back. Good thoughts often get only a corner to stand up in. Anger claims a family pew; sex often gets the whole center section. And what remains is taken up by all the poorer relatives – resentment, hostility, jealousy, and the like. Sympathy, forgiveness, understanding, and their friends are crowded together in a corner where the umbrellas are kept. Such is the strange confusion that is the mind.

Meditation means introducing some order into this confusion. At first, if only for a half hour in meditation, you put up walls and post someone at the door to check for tickets. If a selfish desire comes you may not be able to keep it out, but at least you can say, "Well, there are some broken chairs at the back, and I hope you fall." A medium desire, half selfish, half selfless – what politicians call "enlightened self-interest" – can have seats in the middle section for the time being. And if any selfless desires come, you can say, "Here are the very best seats, front and center – comfortable, with lots of leg room and a little light to read the program by."

In this way your mind becomes orderly. You know where everyone is. If some disorderly thought starts shouting vulgarities at the back of the mind while you are meditating, you know where it comes from and can ask, "Will the gentleman at the back please leave?" Eventually, if we practice meditation sincerely and systematically, all the negative usurpers must go.

In addition to meditation, there is an allied discipline which can also establish peace in the mind. A mantram, or Holy Name, is a powerful spiritual formula which has the capacity to transform consciousness when we repeat it silently in the mind. Quite simply, the mantram gives the mind something to hold on to, something to steady itself by.

Every religious tradition has a mantram, often more than one. For Christians, the name of Jesus itself is a powerful mantram. In Hinduism, among many choices, I recommend *Rama,*

Rama, which was Mahatma Gandhi's mantram, or the longer mantram I received from my own spiritual teacher:

> *Haré Rama Haré Rama,*
> *Rama Rama Haré Haré,*
> *Haré Krishna Haré Krishna,*
> *Krishna Krishna Haré Haré.*

When agitating thoughts like anger, fear, and greed threaten to invade the mind, the mantram is a kind of usher who comes and says, "Excuse me, sir, this seat is reserved for Sympathy. You must have made a mistake." In the early days, if the offending thought refuses to move, all the mantram can do is remind him, "Sir, there are others waiting, and they have been waiting a long time." There is not much power behind the mantram until it gets deeper in consciousness.

The mantram is a proper, polite usher, but meditation is a big, burly bouncer. When you really know how to meditate, you don't tap the thought on the shoulder and say timidly, "Excuse me, but I'm going to have to ask you to leave." You lift the fellow up, open the door, and toss him out. Once meditation deepens, you can do this with any selfish thought, any passion, any craving, any conflict.

To give just one illustration, after you have eaten a big dinner, why should you feel tempted by a midnight snack? It is like somebody coming into the theater after the show is over. "Sorry," you say, "it's time to turn out the lights and lock up." Imagine that desire responding, "I won't go!" Then you call in the bouncer.

When unpleasant thoughts are lounging around all over the place, tossing candy wrappers on the floor and putting their boots up on the upholstery, it's quite exhilarating to be able to say with authority, "Throw them out!" One by one the bouncer pitches them out, and there is an end to the confusion and squalor.

Just as a theater has a ticket collector, we can train the mind to recognize each thought. That is what concentration is for. But when the mind is going fast, we never have a chance to check a thought before it develops momentum in the mind. Civil servants in India used to keep a rubber stamp of their signature in their desks. If they were in a hurry, everything got the rubber stamp. Most of our desires receive the same treatment; we stamp our approval on every one that comes along. The speeded-up mind never guesses it could have a choice.

∗

The Buddha's theory of time, called rather elegantly the "doctrine of momentariness," offers a fascinating explanation of how the mind works. According to this theory, which fits neatly with modern physics, there is no connection between one moment and the next. Each moment is unique and separate. And there is no connection between two thoughts, as can be seen when the mind has been greatly slowed down through the practice of meditation. Of course, this is not at all our everyday perception. We *know* that one thought causes another: I have lost my car key, that makes me feel frustrated, and that makes me want to eat. The connection seems very clear. Yet it is an illusion.

When the mind is really speeding out of control, the same thought begins repeating itself over and over again and thoughts start telescoping into one another. Particularly in people who are upsettable or excitable, one rushing, unfavorable thought pushes another, which pushes another, which pushes another, until we have a whole negative thought-train from stimulus to response.

On the Berkeley campus I once passed the cafeteria in the middle of the morning and saw a student I knew sitting down to a really big breakfast. "What's the matter?" I asked with concern. "Didn't you have time for breakfast in the dorm?"

"Oh, yes," he replied. "I did."

"Then why are you having a second breakfast?"

"Because my biology professor gave me a C minus this morning."

At the risk of being obvious, there is no possible connection between a C minus and a second breakfast. It is all an illusion created by sheer speed. One thought rushes into the mind and announces, "Bad news, old boy. You've blown another assignment." Right on its coattails is another, separate thought, dragged in before you know it: "How horrible!" And hanging on to that thought is a third: "Why not go to the cafeteria and eat it off?"

In all of us the drama is much the same for any compulsive desire: the power of the compulsion comes from the speed of the mind. The application is quite practical. If we can slow the mind down until each thought stops pushing its neighbor, each thought can be free. We will see clearly that there is no connection; so we can intervene between stimulus and response.

Much of the rush of thoughts in the mind comes from unconscious associations. We hear a phrase, smell a fragrance, see a familiar face, and something about it "makes us think" of something else, often setting off a rush of associations in the mind. Marcel Proust, in an extreme instance, goes on for pages about the memories that rush into his mind after a single sip of tea.

We used to play a game in India that never failed to amaze us because of the prolific inventiveness of the mind. In this game, I begin by whispering a sentence to the person sitting next to me. "Steve, I went to the orchard today and saw two apples on a tree." Steve passes it on to John. John whispers it to Brian. Brian whispers it to Tim. And by the time it comes back to me it has become something like, "Easwaran went to Tom's two days ago and got three pears from a fig tree." That is how the mind works; whatever goes in triggers associated thoughts.

For example, right after a political address ask several people to tell you exactly what the speaker said. You will be amazed at how much the answers vary, just because of the different associations that come in. But if you question their accuracy, people will say honestly, "That's what I heard!"

When I was a Boy Scout, one of the tests for the Tenderfoot badge illustrated the same process. Our scoutmaster lined us up in front of a table with a dozen or so objects on it, covered with a table cloth. He removed the cloth for perhaps half a minute, and then he covered it again and asked us to write down all that we had seen. It taught us a good deal about the eccentricities of the human mind. Most of us could remember a decent number of things that were there, and of course we missed some others. But we invariably also wrote down a number of things that were not there. Some boys would even describe their color and size and tell where they lay on the tabletop.

Mainly this was a matter of associations. Where we saw a lock, for example, we might recall a key as well. The thought "lock" would drag in the thought "key," so that when we sat down to write out our report, we actually remembered seeing both. When a boy's imagination was really fertile, he might even add details to his report: "There is a chain for the key, and on the chain a little ivory monkey." My scoutmaster would ask, "Are you sure?" And the boy would reply, "Of course. I have a lock just like that, so I know what the key looks like. And that is the same kind of chain as I have, too."

What we call thinking is often like this. One thought, moving very fast, pushes a dozen other thoughts, and we call the process a reasoned, legitimate, logical response to the situation. If we can slow down the furious activity of the mind – put it in traction and stretch it out –

we find that these thoughts are actually quite distant from each other. Then an upsetting thought will not be able to push the next one. It will just release a little spurt of agitation or excitement or whatever and then die. To use the language of the theater again, even if one agitating thought slips past the ticket collector, we do not have to let in all his friends.

When you look at a length of movie film, it is just a series of separate stills. But when the film is run through a projector, the stills melt together and you get the illusion of continuous motion. The action, in other words, is not in the film; it is created by the speed of the projector.

Just so, the fast mind makes random associations appear inevitable. It is because of the speed of the mind that we get caught up in automatic responses to life. When someone is rude, we think we have to be rude in return. When someone threatens us, we immediately feel angry or afraid.

This movie is what we call our personality. It *is* real, much the same way as a movie is real. But it is not our real Self, and if we could watch it closely we would see that it usually changes from still to still. Most of us think and behave very differently at different times; in effect, our personality changes throughout the day. Even the most dedicated gourmand, for example, has moments when he or she is free from the desire to eat. Similarly, all of us have mornings when we feel secure, certain days when we can shrug our shoulders and take no notice when someone makes an unpleasant joke at our expense. But on certain other days, a little remark rubs us the wrong way and we have to get up from dinner and lock ourselves in the bedroom to watch reruns of *I Love Lucy*.

✳

As long as patience and security come and go like this, they are not too valuable; but on the other hand, it is heartening just to know that they are there. If we can be secure and selfless, even if by fits and starts, we have the capacity, even if it appears only once a month. That capacity is a still in the movie of the mind. As concentration deepens, we can stretch the still into an episode. And if it can come once a month, why not encourage it to come once a week? Why not once a day? Once an hour? Finally we are able to continue it without any break at all.

This is primarily a matter of learning to direct and hold attention. Without the training of meditation, very few of us have much natural control over our attention. As a result, when someone is unkind to us, we cannot help brooding on that person's words and actions. On the bus, though we try to concentrate on the newspaper, the same harsh phrases keep running through our minds. At dinner, even with good food in front of us, we cannot forget the look in the other person's eyes. And at night, though it is painful, we fall asleep remembering the disdainful curl of his lip. We may even replay the incident in dreams, or concoct scenes of angry retaliation.

In all this, attention is scarcely in the here and now. We are actually living in the past, in a time and place that are utterly unreal. The evidence is that if someone asks for the time, we will not hear; when we go to bed, we may not remember what we ate for dinner. Our attention is trapped in a private never-never land.

Attention could be an immensely significant field of study, yet it has been explored in depth only by those rare men and women who have practiced spiritual disciplines. In training the mind to dwell with complete attention on God, they have gained one of the most precious skills a human being can have: when the mind is dwelling on some past wrong or tragedy, they can turn their attention away from the past and bring the mind completely into the present.

When we can do this, the whole burden of the past falls away: not only the weight of others' wrongs, but also of our own previous mistakes. That is what real forgiveness means, and why Saint Francis of Assisi says, "It is in pardoning that we are pardoned." It sounds impossible, but Saint Teresa, Saint Francis, Mahatma Gandhi, and many others in all religions testify with humility yet utter honesty, "We have done it. Therefore, you can too."

In meditation, we learn this skill by bringing

our attention back to the words of an inspira-
tional passage whenever it strays away. I have
included a section about the practice of meditation in the appendix, but here I would simply
like to explain how meditation can train attention. Attention is like a restless puppy, fond of
running after anything new that comes along.
When it sees an intensely charged memory, it
cannot let it roll by. It has to chase the memory
and keep yapping, yapping, yapping. Just as
with a dog, we have to call the mind back over
and over again whenever we sit down for meditation. This may go on for years. But if we keep
practicing diligently and systematically, the day
will come when we can put our attention
where we want it without effort, and it will stay
without any movement or protest. Then, however unkind somebody may have been, we cannot be resentful. Our attention will not turn to
the past at all.

Nor will it dwell on the future, in fears,
hopes, and anxieties. The future is no more real
than the past. Isn't there a saying, "Don't trouble trouble till trouble troubles you"?

Many of the things we worry about do not

even materialize. My spiritual teacher used to point this out to me whenever I got anxious over some mountain that turned out to be a molehill. "See?" she would say in her loving manner. "The things you were so afraid of did not come true."

Dwelling on things under the compulsion of anxiety or fear magnifies life's little problems out of all proportion. When the mind is trained, you can lift it gently out of such compulsions and bring it back completely to the present.

When attention is one hundred percent in the present, without a wisp in the past or future, there is no longer any time. And when there is no time, there is no death. We have escaped at last from the dominion of death, from the valley of the shadow of death. As the great mystics of all religions put it, we are delivered out of time into the eternal Now. To rest completely on each present moment like this, without any past or future, floods our hearts with joy – a million times more joy than any pleasure of the senses can bring.

The Buddha illustrated the illusion of time with the example of a torch, the same kind of torch we used in Kerala when I was growing up. We didn't have electricity in the village in those days, and of course we didn't have cinemas. For entertainment we sometimes went to a neighboring village two or three miles away to see a play based on a story from one of India's epics. The performance would begin after sunset on an open-air stage and part of our enjoyment was just being out under the tropical sky in the cool of the evening.

However, the road to and from this village skirted a forest where wild animals roamed. Wild animals are not a welcome attraction after dark, so to keep them away as much as to light our path, we boys made torches from dry coconut fronds and whirled them around before us as we walked. From a distance you would not see coconut fronds or boys whirling them in their hands; you would see only circles of fire moving through the night.

As long as the torch is whirling swiftly, the Buddha said, you see a circle of fire. But when the whirling stops, the circle disappears. Then you see what is really there: a simple fiber torch. In exactly the same way, it is because the mind is being swirled around faster and faster that we see things that are not there. Resentments, for example, are not there. They are in the past, and the past is a mirage, just as the future is a camouflage.

When the body, senses, mind, intellect, and ego become still, we see life as it is – whole, indivisible, divine. "Be still," the Bible says, "and know that I am God." We no longer see this figment of whirling, separate circles. We see there is only One on earth, masquerading as many: the Lord of Love disguised as over five billion men, women, and children.

The mystics ask, Who is there on earth but God? In this mystic domain, when we enter the kingdom of heaven within, we are out of time; we are lifted completely beyond the reach of death. We live wholly in the present moment – in "eternity's sunrise," as William Blake said, in the day that never ends.

The Lesson of the Lilac

*I go, the first of many who will die, in the
midst of many who are dying, on a mission to
Death. See how it was with those who came
before, how it will be with those who are
living: like corn mortals ripen and fall; like
corn they come up again.*

—The Upanishads

Outside my window there is a lilac bush which I
see every morning at breakfast. A month ago I
had only to open the window to smell its heady
perfume, and for two or three weeks it was in
opulent blossom. Then one day I looked out and
noticed that the delicate flowers had turned
brown. Their fragrance no longer filled the air.
How quickly it was over! For me it wasn't a lesson in gardening. It was a very personal message

telling me, "Let these lilacs remind you that all things flourish and then fade."

Nothing in life is more pressing than learning to face death. If we could live for a thousand years, there would be no urgency in this lesson. We could devote a hundred years to making money, and when this failed to bring us happiness we would still have plenty of time. We could devote another hundred years to attaining fame and another hundred to pursuing the pleasures of the senses, and when we had carefully explored all these blind alleys, we would still have the time and the vitality to change our direction and look for the source of lasting security and joy that is within each of us. But the tragedy is that we have very little time to make this discovery.

I once read a story about a man who kept putting off life's deeper questions in order to have just one more fling, to make just one more deal. Time after time he told himself that next week, or next month, or next year, he would change his life.

Then, one night, he dreamed that he was dying. There was no chance now to change his direction. Time had run out on him, and all his plans for making a new start in life could never be fulfilled. It was a terrifying experience, and as he struggled to wake up, he vowed passionately not to postpone for a single morning more. But when he tried to sit up, he found it was no dream; he *was* on his deathbed.

It is a sobering story. Most of us have a tendency to postpone in just this way. Once we have finished painting the kitchen, we say, once we have finished our dissertation, once we have paid off our loan, then we will have time to devote ourselves to what is really important. But when the kitchen has been painted and the dissertation has been turned in, there will still be letters to write, checkbooks to balance, garages to clean, places to go and people to see. So the Buddhist mystic Milarepa advises, "The affairs of business will drag on forever. Do not delay the search for truth."

No one would deny that the body will grow old someday, that sooner or later it must fail and drop away. But to judge from our behavior, very few of us really believe that this is ever going to happen to *us*. Have you noticed that drivers on the highway slow down when they pass the scene of a serious accident? For an instant, while the evidence is before our eyes, there comes the sobering realization: "That could have happened to me!" Yet only a few minutes later we are driving along at top speed again, the reminder of mortality forgotten. It is the same when a member of our family dies, or a friend, or for that matter our dog. Even the death of an utter stranger, reported on the back page of the morning paper, can penetrate the routine of our lives with the same insistent message: "Stop! Remember! It is over so soon." We reflect on it a minute, but soon we are going about business as usual, skimming along on the surface of life, forgetful that in the end death is waiting for us all.

As we grow older and the body begins to register the signs of aging, reminders of life's transiency are more and more frequent. Past the midpoint of our lives, when the pursuits and ambitions of our youth begin to lose some of their glamour, the speed at which life goes by is seen more clearly. Just yesterday, it seems, we were in high school; today we are watching our son graduate from college. We remember being a newlywed as if it were last weekend, and today we are putting the third candle on our granddaughter's birthday cake. Like the lilac, like the death of a loved one or a friend, all these are reminders that it is time to wake up from the dream that money or pleasure or prestige can make us happy, time to wake up and discover why it is that we have come into this life.

When the alarm clock is ringing, when a voice inside is saying, "You know you're not getting any younger," the last thing to do is to pull the blankets up over our heads and try to fall asleep again. But most of us seem to want to sleep on as long as we can. Our response to the body's aches and pains, to the little wrinkles and gray hairs, is to try to hide them and pretend they are not there. We take a couple of aspirin, smooth on more cosmetics, double our dosage of vitamin E, distract ourselves with travel or social life or some new sport, as if by not thinking about it we could escape death's notice forever.

In the modern world we have compounded our natural inclination to isolate ourselves from death. Despite the current emphasis on "death and dying," hospitals and nursing homes still hide death from us, and instead we are exposed to unreal images of ageless youth on television and in films.

To take one example of this avoidance, I think it is the reason why many people who think of themselves as fond of animals never stop to think how many creatures are killed to provide some of the luxuries they enjoy. Because death is not real to them, they are insensitive to the suffering of animals who are slaughtered for their skins or fur or tusks. People are simply not aware. Just last week a young woman I was talking to, describing the bitter cold of New York City, mentioned with a twinge of envy a friend's coat which was completely lined in fox fur. Neither she nor her friend, I am sure, were aware that fox fur actually comes from a fox that would prefer to wear its coat itself.

Death should never be faceless; death is always personal. Whether it is someone in our home, a child on the other side of the globe, or one of God's creatures like a fox or a raccoon, all of us love life; all of us fear death. This is the unity that binds us all together, and as our eyes begin to open to it, we shall see life's transiency everywhere we go.

In my village we were reminded of this every year at the onset of the monsoon. As the rains began, the sky would be filled with thousands and thousands of moths. These moths live only for two or three hours, but they come like the locusts in the biblical plague; you cannot even yawn without running the risk of getting one in your mouth. For just a short while they are everywhere, and then, suddenly, they are gone. Their lives are spent in just a fraction of a day.

Look at the sense of time these moths must have. "Give us a calendar," they would say, "for just two and a half hours. Give us a clock for one hundred and fifty minutes to last us from birth to death." Half a minute would be a year to them; the hundredth part of a second would be as precious as a day is to us. If we were to tell them that we live hundreds of thousands of times longer, they would not even be able to grasp the scope of it. Yet from a cosmic point of view our bodies are no more eternal than these moths, who come and go in a matter of hours.

The spiritual teachers of all religions remind us that at this very minute the messengers of death are on their way with a letter for each of us. This letter was posted the day we were born, and we never know when it will arrive. For some the letter takes a long time to reach its destination; for others it comes by special delivery at midnight. It shocks us to hear about the sudden death of a friend in an auto accident, just as it shocks us to hear that someone has a terminal illness with only two or three years to live. But the truth is that the body is mortal, and whether it lasts five years or fifty is only a matter of degree.

This whole universe is a theater of death. Everything that has been created is in the process of passing away. For the monsoon moth it is a matter of hours; towards the other end of the scale there is the sun, which has been blazing away in the sky for much longer than there has been life on our earth. It is difficult to imagine that the sun has not been around forever.

Yet like us, our sun has a kind of birthday too. He was born some six billion years ago out of contracting clouds of gas, and though he seems fit enough now – just right to sustain life on earth – he has already entered middle age. Gradually the vital fusion fires at his core are going to cool and then flare up erratically as he swells into a "red giant," a lethargic solar Falstaff with a middle-age bulge that engulfs the earth. After another ten billion years, when his temperature drops for the last time, he will explode in a final display of solar dramatics or suddenly begin to contract and cool until he is no more than another cold cinder floating in space.

Against this vast life cycle, only the universe could seem eternal. Yet even that may have an end. According to one current theory, just as the universe was born in an unimaginable explosion from a single point before there was either space or time, it will eventually collapse into a point again and disappear, pulling its grave in after it. The Hindu scriptures say that there have been countless universes like this and there will be countless more hereafter, in an endless cycle of creation, expansion, and destruction. In the language of the Buddha, the whole of creation is an endless process of birth and death.

The miracle that all the world's great religions affirm is that you and I can break out of this cycle of birth and death once and for all. My spiritual teacher, my grandmother, had her own ways of teaching me this when I was still quite small. I was always an enthusiastic student, and because I loved my granny very much, I used to run home every day to tell her what I had learned. And every day she would be waiting for me right by the front gate. Once, however, I must have come home with gloom showing on my face, because Granny immediately asked what was the matter. "Bad news, Granny," I said. "Today in geography our teacher told us that compared to the universe, you and I are no more than specks of dust."

Granny was a simple village woman, but she was never one to be intimidated by booklearning. She laughed and took me by the hand. "Look," she said, pointing up at the sky. "Even that sun is going to burn out someday and pass away. But you and I, because the Lord lives in us, can never die."

Of course, the body must wear out and fall away someday; no one would deny it. But you and I are not the body. As the Sufi mystic Abu Hamid al-Ghazali avowed in a little poem composed on his deathbed:

> When my friends weep over my dead body,
> Ask them, "Do you mistake him to be this?"
> Tell them I swear in the name of the Lord
> That this dead body is not I. It was
> My garment while I lived on earth,
> I wore it during my stay there.

In my youth I did not understand this attitude toward death, but today, because of many years of spiritual disciplines, I have learned not to identify myself with what is changing. I have a brown jacket with a Nehru collar, made in India, which I take very good care of. I expect it to last me for many more years, but when it is no longer presentable I am going to give it away without any feelings of regret. It has served me well, but it is in the nature of a jacket to wear out. Similarly, this body of mine is another brown jacket made in India – it has the label of its Maker right inside. I take good care of it too, but when the time comes, I will be able to take it off without any break in consciousness.

In the Bhagavad Gita this is enunciated in very clear terms:

> As a person abandons worn-out clothes and acquires new ones, so when the body is worn out a new body is acquired by the Self, who lives within.

*

At the time of death, the Hindu scriptures say, the soul does not depart from the body suddenly. It takes its jackets off step by step. There is a gradual withdrawal of consciousness from the senses into the mind and then from the mind into the Self. Only then does the Self depart.

First, the doors of the senses shut completely, and external awareness of the body and of our surroundings is gone. At this stage, the dying person ceases to hear or see anything in the external world because consciousness has been withdrawn from the ears and the eyes. Yet even though there is no experience of external sensations, there is still consciousness in the mind, with all its desires and regrets, all its conflicts and hopes and fears.

At this point there is no longer a surface level of consciousness; there are no random thoughts. The content of our consciousness will be whatever we have dwelt upon most, whatever we have worked hardest for, whatever we have desired most intensely. And when the Self departs from the body, it is this core of consciousness that accompanies it into the next life. That is why the Upanishads say:

We are what our deep, driving desire is.
As our deep, driving desire is, so is our will.
As our will is, so is our deed.
As our deed is, so is our destiny.

What occupies our consciousness at the moment of death, therefore, is of the utmost importance. In India a scripture like the Bhagavad Gita is read aloud while a person is dying, so that something of its message will be with that person in his or her final moments. Very much the same thing is done in other major religions. Even more effective in this critical transition is for the dying person to repeat the mantram over and over in the mind.

The mantram is always a powerful ally, and it is especially comforting at the time of death. When I have had occasion to sit by the side of someone who is dying, I just repeat my mantram silently. There is no need to talk at such times; simply holding that person's hand and repeating the mantram, especially when there is a bond of love between you, can help a great deal to calm the turbulence that may overtake the mind at the time of death.

This is the advice that the great mystics of all religious traditions have given us: to call upon God at the time of death. Whatever mantram we use, we are calling upon a power not without but within. The Lord is not a figure in a distant galaxy, but a divine presence that abides in our hearts as our real Self.

For most people, the onset of death precipitates a terrible sense of deprivation. All the attachments we have formed over a lifetime, all our cravings for sensory experience, tie us to the body. Then, when death comes, there is a terrible struggle when it tears us away – and the harder we cling, the more it will hurt.

My grandmother had a vivid way of getting this point across. Once, as a child, I asked her why death should involve so much suffering. She didn't answer; she just told me to sit in one of our big wooden chairs and hold on with all my strength. Then she tried to pull me out of the chair. I held on for all I was worth, but my granny was a strong woman, and with one painful wrench she had me on my feet. "That hurt!" I said.

"Now sit down again," she said, "but this time don't hold on." I did as she said, and there was no struggle, no pain; she raised me gently into her arms.

This is the secret of facing death. When death comes and growls that our time has come, we just say, "You don't have to growl. I'm ready to come on my own." Then we take off the jacket that is the body, hand it over carefully, and go to our real home.

✳

Once my grandmother came very close to death. She had cholera, and everyone, including the doctor, thought she had only a few hours to live. She had even given instructions about the funeral pyre, requesting that no mango wood be used because its acrid smoke would irritate the mourners' eyes. Even in death she was thinking of the comfort of others.

I was a child then, and because my love for her was so great, I was sent upstairs to be away from the scene of death. At dawn I was brought down to take leave of her. A tremendous feeling of desertion swept over me. "Granny, you can't die!" I cried. "What will happen to me without you?"

A few hours later, instead of breathing her last, my grandmother sat up on her bed with great difficulty and asked my mother to bring her a pot of strong tea. There is no doubt in my mind that it was my deep desire for her loving guidance, and her equally deep desire to help me, that enabled her to pull herself back from death to continue her work as my spiritual teacher. People with spiritual awareness do not live for themselves alone; they live because they feel they have a contribution to make to life. For such great souls, death is not just a matter of gracefully giving up the body and personal attachments; it means going home after completing their work on earth.

In India there is no more inspiring example than that of the Compassionate Buddha, who shed his body at the age of eighty after a long, fruitful life teaching the Noble Eightfold Path that leads to the end of sorrow. He was a vigorous teacher right up to a brief spell of illness just before he breathed his last. When his disciples gathered around him, all his concern was for their welfare. In his final words he told them, "Be lamps unto yourselves. Work out your salvation with diligence." And he told them not to be discouraged because he would no longer be with them in the physical body. In Sri Lanka, at Anuradhapura, one can see a beautiful representation of this scene sculpted in rock. Lying peacefully on his side, just embarking on his final release from the cycle of birth and death, the Buddha is giving his last instructions to his grieving disciple Ananda, showing him the way to immortality.

The records of the Christian tradition, too, are full of inspiring accounts of how mortal men and women can face the challenge of death in calmness and with faith. We can read the account of Teresa of Avila's death, and nearer to our own times we have the story of Thérèse of Lisieux. Those who witnessed their final moments say that both were exalted in their deaths and died in states of mystical awareness. According to her biographer, Saint Teresa said near the end, "My Lord, now is the time to set forth: may it be very soon, and may your most holy will be accomplished. Now the hour has come for me to leave this exile, and my soul rejoices at one with you for what I have so desired."

Even ordinary people like you and me can face our last hours with understanding and courage if we practice spiritual disciplines with real earnestness. If we begin now to repeat the mantram, and repeat it whenever we get an opportunity, it will be there when we need it even in the turmoil of the body's final hours. Even though our repetition may seem mechanical to begin with, if we practice meditation earnestly and support our meditation with a program of spiritual living, the mantram will enable us to go deeper and deeper into our consciousness. Practice is the important thing, and sustained enthusiasm.

The mantram is the raft to carry us across the sea of death to the other shore. Together, meditation and the mantram can establish us in the state of spiritual awareness. Once we realize God, we are united with him forever. Our constant awareness of the unity of life, our constant awareness of the divine presence within, is not interrupted even when the physical body falls away. Sri Krishna gives us this promise in the Bhagavad Gita:

> . . . they for whom I am the goal supreme,
> Who do all work renouncing self for me,
> Meditate on me with single-hearted
> Devotion – these will I swiftly rescue
> From the fragment's cycle of birth and death
> To fullness of eternal life in me.

This is what Jesus means when he promises us life everlasting: "Verily, verily I say unto you,

If a man keep my saying, he shall never see death."

In my early years in this country, though many earnest men and women came regularly to my talks on meditation, I don't think they paid much attention to what I said about immortality. That death is not inevitable, that it can be conquered, and that this conquest has to be achieved here in this life – these are things that are beyond all reason, beyond the imagination, beyond any mundane possibility. When spiritual teachers say that going beyond time means going beyond death, we usually think they are speaking figuratively. Very few of us are prepared to accept that this means immortality as *immortality*: a literal, attainable state. Yet our love of adventure, our capacity for daring, our rebelliousness, and our passions can all be rechanneled to release within us the extraordinary energy required to realize immortality here and now.

The Great Awakening

Hence, in a season of calm weather
Though inland far we be,
Our Souls have sight of that immortal sea
Which brought us hither,
Can in a moment travel thither,
And see the Children sport upon the shore,
And hear the mighty waters rolling evermore.

> −William Wordsworth,
> "Intimations of Immortality"

Twenty-five hundred years ago the Compassionate Buddha attained enlightenment at the age of thirty two. He spent the rest of his life walking the dusty roads of northern India, teaching the way that leads to the end of suffering and death. Once, when he was seated with his disciples on the outskirts of a small town, a woman named Kisha Gotami made her way through the crowd and knelt at his feet. Her tear-streaked face was wild with grief, and in the fold of her sari she carried a tiny child.

"I've been to everyone," she pleaded, "but still my son will not move, will not breathe. Can't you save him? Can't the Blessed One work miracles?"

"I can help you, sister," the Buddha promised. "But first I will need a handful of mustard seed – and it must come from a house where no one has died."

With hope reborn in her heart, Kisha Gotami turned back to the village and stopped at the first house. The woman who met her was full of understanding. "Of course I will give you some mustard seed! How much does the Blessed One need to work his miracle?"

"Just a little," Kisha Gotami said. Then, remembering suddenly: "But it must come from a house where no one has died."

The woman answered with a smile of pity. "Many have died here. Just last month I lost my grandfather."

Kisha Gotami lowered her eyes, "I'm sorry. I'll try next door."

But next door it was the same – and at the

next house, and the next, and the house after that. Everyone wanted to help, but no one could meet that one simple condition. Death had come to all.

Finally Kisha Gotami understood. She took her child to the cremation ground and returned to the Compassionate Buddha.

"Sister," he greeted her, "did you bring me the mustard seed?"

"Blessed One," she said, "I have understood. Please let me be your disciple."

So Kisha Gotami became the disciple of the Buddha, and he taught her the way that leads beyond suffering and death. "For those struggling in midstream in great fear of the flood, of growing old and of dying – for all those I say an island exists where there is no place for impediments, no place for clinging: the island of no going beyond. I call it nirvana, the complete destruction of old age and dying."

Thus Kisha Gotami began the long journey of spiritual awakening.

The Buddha called himself *Tathagata*, "he who has gone this way," because he wanted everyone to know that he was human: a mortal who had struggled just as they struggled, who had suffered but had finally reached the goal. He was human, yet he had achieved what so few achieve: he had awakened himself from the long dream of separateness and death that we call everyday experience. People called him the Buddha because he was awake – the literal, etymological meaning of the word *buddha,* from the root *budh,* "to wake up." He was awake while others slept. And his whole teaching was simply about one thing: trying to wake them up, too.

The Buddha never theorized, and he never relied on external authority. That is one reason why he appeals to so many of us in the modern world.

The Buddha's is a scientific view of life, fulfilling the rigorous requirements of scientific thought. He states the hypothesis that underneath the constant flux and passing phenomena of life, where all is change, there is an underlying reality that is changeless, not affected by time, place, circumstance, decay, or death. And if you ask him, "Blessed One, what is the proof of this?" he will become the scientist and say,

"Why don't you perform the experiment yourself? Put on your lab coat, get into your lab, and look." And he adds, "These are the eight steps that you have to follow in performing this experiment: right understanding, right aspiration, right speech, right conduct, right occupation, right effort, right mindfulness, and right meditation."

Among the Buddha's followers there was an intelligent, well-informed, but not entirely well mannered disciple named Malunkyaputra, who was always asking speculative questions. We might say he was a kind of graduate student.

Once, when the Blessed One was talking about nirvana, Malunkyaputra raised his hand.

"Blessed One, is there a soul before birth? Is there a soul after death? If there is no soul after death, what is left?" He went on and on like this. The Buddha listened patiently and then said with compassion, "Malunkyaputra, there once was a soldier who was mortally wounded on the battlefield by a poisoned arrow. The surgeon rushed to help him, but as he started to pull the arrow out the soldier stopped him. 'Doctor,' he said, 'before you take this arrow out, I want to know about the man who shot it. Was he tall or short? Was he brown or black? From what kind of family does he come?'"

At this point the Buddha must have smiled at Malunkyaputra when he said, "The doctor told the soldier, 'I can find out all this for you and answer all your questions, but before I have done so you would have gone into another incarnation.'"

I imagine that the Buddha said this with such sweetness that for once Malunkyaputra was silenced. Seeing understanding dawning in his disciple's eyes, the Buddha pressed his point home. "The religious life, Malunkyaputra, does not depend on the dogma that the world is eternal; nor does the religious life depend on the dogma that the world is not eternal. Whether these dogmas obtain or not, there still remain birth, old age, death, sorrow, lamentation, misery, grief, and despair. It is for the extinction of these in the present life that I am prescribing the Noble Eightfold Path."

On most occasions when he was asked speculative questions, the Buddha observed what tradition calls a "noble silence." It is not that he could not answer these questions or that they are not intriguing, but there is literally no time in life to pursue all the beckoning avenues of spiritual and philosophical inquiry. As the Buddha put it so bluntly but so gently, we will be dead long before we come to the end of our wearisome searches.

Once, in my early days in this country, I was introduced to a distinguished scholar who took me to see his library. I was amazed at the number of books he had on meditation from all kinds of traditions.

"I had no idea you had such a deep interest in the subject of meditation," I said. "You must be meditating long hours every day."

He coughed. "Actually," he said, "I don't have any time for meditation. I'm too busy reading all these books." Then he asked me, "You must be familiar with most of these?"

I too tried to cough. "No," I confessed, "I don't have time for reading books on meditation. I just meditate."

This is the message of the Buddha: instead of reading about meditation, practice it. As the Upanishads say, "Arise! Awake! Seek out the path to immortality." This path is long and hard, but even with our first steps the desires of the human heart begin to be fulfilled.

✳

Over all the transience of life reigns an immutable power that governs all the natural forces in the cosmos. "At the command of that power," the Upanishads say, "fire burns, the sun shines, stars glow, the wind blows, and death stalks about to kill." This divine creative power, called by many names in the world's religions, is the supreme magician who creates this passing play of life and death.

Some years ago I took a few friends to an excellent magic show. We had seats in the middle of the theater, but a young friend named Josh went and stood right near the stage to be able to expose the magician. Not only did he not succeed, but the magician managed to impress Josh even more than the rest of us.

He began by bringing ordinary little creatures out of his top hat – rabbits, hamsters, doves, the usual contents of a magician's hat.

Josh was about to yawn when the animals suddenly got bigger and more offbeat: owls, vultures, a couple of overfed poodles. By the time he brought out a full-grown horse, everybody was sitting up and taking proper notice. He threw a large red blanket over the horse, and when he whipped it away the animal was gone. There was consternation on Josh's young face.

It is the same with the cosmic magic of birth and death. In Sanskrit, the passing show of life – the illusion that we are all separate creatures rather than an indivisible divine whole – is called *maya*, with which the English word *magic* may be connected. Out of apparent nothingness God brings you and me and all these innumerable creatures out upon the stage. Then, all too soon, he sweeps us away. Those with whom we have grown up, gone to school, shared the joys and trials of our adult years – one by one they just go.

Once the Supreme Magician throws the blanket of *maya* over us, when he lifts it again we are gone – but only so long as we identify ourselves with what is passing. We don't have to disappear. If we can learn to identify ourselves with the Self, when the blanket is removed we will still be one with the magician himself, the Lord.

In the climax of meditation called *samadhi,* when the mind becomes still, we see the world as it is – as Angela of Foligno says, "full of God." Swami Ramdas of South India, whom my wife and I met, is even more daring. The world is not only full of God, he says; "the world *is* God." This is not a philosophical vision. When you reach this state, you will see this divinity in everyone, everywhere you look – though you will also see, at the same time, how thick are the layers of ignorance that cover this divinity within us.

By contrast, how sorrowful the world seems through purely physical eyes! Bertrand Russell, whom I admired as a student for his idealism and courage, chilled my heart with his personal summary: "Brief and powerless is man's life. On him and all his race the slow, sure doom falls, pitiless and dark." And Matthew Arnold wrote hauntingly that the world

Hath really neither joy, nor love, nor light,
Nor certitude, nor peace, nor help for pain;

And we are here as on a darkling plain
Swept with confused alarms of struggle
    and flight
Where ignorant armies clash by night.

Thomas Hardy, a brilliant novelist, once declared that life is a desert with one or two oases. The mystics would say no: life is an opportunity to learn, to serve, and to love. On the one hand, we have Matthew Arnold saying we live without light "on a darkling plain"; on the other, we have the moving testimony of Saint Teresa of Avila: "I live in a light that knows no night." The choice is ours: to continue to sleep in the world of night, or to wake up into the world of light.

Swami Ramdas gives us good spiritual counsel:

Live always in the awareness of your immortal life. Let this consciousness never leave you in all the vicissitudes of life. All things that are visible pass away. All events that happen dissolve in the past. The eternal reality, which is your real nature, is alone permanent. . . . Why pursue merely the shadows of life when eternity can be yours?

✳

How are we, then, to wake ourselves up? Saint Thomas Aquinas tells us:

> Three things are necessary for salvation: to know what we ought to believe, to know what we ought to desire, to know what we ought to do.

The scriptures and mystics of all religions concur on what to believe: that the core of our personality is divine, and that the purpose of life is to discover this divinity for ourselves. What to desire, then, is God himself, which is why mastery of desire has been called the key to Self-realization. Meditation enables us to withdraw our desires from frustrating, ephemeral channels and redirect them toward Self-realization in an overwhelming, overriding flood of longing to be united with our real Self forever. To use the traditional language of mysticism, this is entering the kingdom of heaven, in which we realize our union with God in a marriage that can never be broken.

When this is understood, the third requirement – what we ought to do in life – becomes clear. It is the Self within who enables us to do the job that every human being has come into life to do: to become aware of who we really are and go beyond death once and for all. When that is done, the Upanishads say, everything has been done. "When you know the Self, every-thing in life is known," because it is this Self that is the essence of all things.

The implication is unavoidable: until we dis-cover the Self, no matter how successful we may have been by ordinary standards, we have failed in our main job. Making money, collect-ing pleasures, visiting exotic places, making a name for ourselves – these are not our real job. They only leave us hungrier than we were be-fore, more alienated, more lonely.

When we are young, most of us naturally find it difficult to grasp the transience of things. It is only as we grow older that we begin to un-derstand the words of Marcus Aurelius: "Time is a sort of river of passing events, and strong is its current. No sooner is a thing brought to sight than it is swept by and another takes its place, and this too will be swept away." And he adds, almost in the language of the Buddha: "The universe is change; our life is what our thoughts make it."

The classic Hindu pattern of life divides our lifetime into four periods. The first and second are the student and householder periods: these two comprise, roughly, the first half of life. The third and fourth periods – retirement and detachment – together form the second half of life. According to this concept, during the second half of life many changes in attitude have to be brought about, not by anyone outside but by ourselves. These far-reaching changes may sound harsh, but when practiced they become beneficial and supportive; for they are in accordance with the natural rhythm of life. As Saint Paul puts it, "When I was a child, I spake as a child, I thought as a child, I understood as a child; but when I became a man, I put away childish things."

Once we enter the second half of life, we should begin to realize that there is not a day to waste – not a day to quarrel, not a day to brood upon ourselves. One day wasted means one day more given to death; one day gained means one day less for death. Our whole outlook should become that of a determined, trained runner who is prepared to beat death whatever the price.

I am going to be realistic now. There *will* be times when death appears to be gaining on you: when you get seriously ill, for example, or in a depression when your hopes are low. At such times, look upon it as an opponent gaining on you in a race. Instead of being discouraged or giving up, train yourself more. That is what I did. Whenever a dear relative or friend would die, it was as if death were gaining upon me. I could almost feel his hot breath down my collar. And I would rededicate myself to my training, doing everything possible to deepen my meditation.

The third stage of the Hindu model – that is, the beginning of the second half of life – is called, literally, "retiring to the forest." Today, of course, "retirement" means the time when we no longer have to go to the office or the store or the factory. We may think it means a chance to move to a warmer climate or go on a long vacation. When people speak to me about

their retirement plans and ask when I plan to retire myself, I want to ask, "Retire from what?
Retire from life?" I never intend to retire. I want
to go on making a contribution to life right up
until my last day. That is what I recommend to
everyone, for it will mean a longer and a much
more meaningful life. After all, even if we no
longer join the rush hour traffic every morning,
that doesn't mean our capacity to contribute to
life is any less. In fact, "retirement" may mean
that we can now contribute more to our family,
to our neighborhood, to our city, to our country, to our world. It may mean we have more
time to give to meditation and other spiritual
disciplines.

In spirit, the Hindu concept of retirement
means withdrawing from identification with
the body – a capacity which is little known in
our modern world. Many older people now
speak of how they want to be teenagers again,
able to stay up late at a party and turn up fresh as
the dew the next morning. But we can school
ourselves to think in another way. Instead of a
capacity for party-going, we can cultivate more
useful resources: we can be more patient than

we were before; we can be more selfless; we can help people more; we can support people more. That is the real meaning of retirement.

This is what the second half of life is for, and if I may say so, it will give us a richer personality than we had during the first half of life. This growth in spiritual awareness eventually becomes what in Sanskrit is called *sannyasa:* detachment, the fourth and final stage, which is the fruit of spiritual disciplines. Utter detachment does not come easily to anybody, but it yields great benefits.

✳

Partly, this detachment is from material things. In our early days, most of us probably took a certain amount of pleasure in possessions – clothes, cars, houses, gadgets of all kinds. But it is not uncommon for such attractions to lose some of their glamour when we enter our forties or fifties. When we were younger, attachments to all these material things perhaps did not do us a great deal of harm, but in the latter half of life, no amount of material possessions is going to protect us from the depression and sense of futility that advancing years often bring.

I am not recommending poverty. I am not suggesting that we leave our car at the Goodwill, sell the house, and move into a cave. The important thing is to have what we need for a comfortable life without being owned by our possessions, and without being driven by the compulsion to acquire more and more. For though they can create a certain facade, no amount of wealth or material things can hold off the changes that time is going to bring to all of us.

In this matter, a judicious Greek philosopher gives good spiritual advice. "Remember," Epictetus said, "to behave in life as you would behave at a banquet. When something is being passed around, as it comes to you, stretch out your hand and take a portion of it politely. When it passes on, do not try to hold on to it; when it has not yet come to you, do not reach out for it with your desire but wait until it presents itself. So act toward children, toward spouse, toward office, toward wealth." That is the secret of detachment.

Epictetus would have been at home at a Hindu banquet, for we have three unwritten rules. One is that there is a regular apportionment of space on the piece of banana leaf that serves as a plate. You don't pile things on top of each other; each dish is served in a particular order in its appropriate place. Second, when something delicious is set in front of you, you don't start eating immediately; you wait until everybody has been served. Children get so impatient that a mother sometimes has to slap their wrists gently; but by the age of five or so, all are able to sit patiently waiting until the serving is done and everyone observes a few moments' repetition of the mantram. After that, conversation stops; the only sounds you hear are of eating and drinking. And the third rule is that when you are done, you have to wait until the last person has finished the last bite before you get up. This unwritten code of banana-plate manners makes even the largest family feast go smoothly.

But being detached from material possessions is the easy part. Now comes the hard part: freedom from possessive attachments to people. The highest kind of love is impersonal: that is, it shines equally on all, alike on friend and foe, as the Bhagavad Gita and the Buddha and Jesus the Christ all make clear. That is the terribly hard thing for us to understand, and it has been one of the hardest lessons for me to learn. I have always been a person with passionate loyalties and a capacity for wholehearted devotion in my relationships, and to learn not to restrict that devotion to a few individuals was a long and painful process.

When our love is no longer restricted to one or two people, however, all our depth of love is free to flow toward everyone and every creature. Then, to use the language of mysticism, the lover of God becomes love itself.

As we enter the second half of life, if we are sensitive, we will begin to suspect that we cannot put our trust in any changing relationship based on physical attraction, or even in a relationship based on sympathy of mind or intellect. All these shift and alter with the passage of time. The only relationship that is permanent is the relationship between the Self in you and the same Self in others: the spiritual relationship in which we forget ourselves in living for the welfare of all. As the Upanishads say,

> A wife loves her husband not for his own sake, but because the Self lives in him. A husband loves his wife not for her own sake, but because the Self lives in her. Children are loved not for their own sake, but because the Self lives in them. All creatures are loved not for their own sake, but because the Self lives in them.

In personal relationships we should try to observe the kind of restraint Epictetus recommends. Don't try to cling to people and hold them to you: everything changes, and if you try to arrest relationships and hold on to others, making them conform to your own needs, the light of love is extinguished very soon. This is the real meaning of detachment. It's not running away from life, but having no particular, private, personal attachments: not the absence of love but the fullness of love for all.

The word *detachment* has a cold sound in English, but it is only when we have this kind of perfect spiritual detachment that our compassion extends to every creature. We will see in the death of any creature the fate of us all.

"Never send to know for whom the bell tolls; it tolls for thee," as John Donne said. Whenever any creature or any person dies, we lose a part of ourselves.

The key to this universal compassion is given in the Gita: "beyond the reach of 'I and mine.'" If you want to ascend the highest peak that a human being can climb, this is one of the most agonizing qualifications: no sense of "mine" at all, neither with things nor with people. And as if that weren't enough, the Gita adds "not a trace of *ahamkara*." *Ahamkara* is one of those simple yet profound Sanskrit words that it is impossible to translate into English. Made up of two smaller words, *aham,* "I," and *kara,* "maker," it implies egotism and self-will: in general, too great a measure of self-regard and too great a following after our own passions and inclinations. Sannyasa, perfect detachment, ultimately means detachment from our own selfish impulses and inclinations.

The remedy for ahamkara, in the Buddha's language, is *nirvana,* from *nir,* "out," and *vana,* "to blow." You keep blowing for years and years and one day the fire of selfishness goes out. You don't snuff it out in one day; you have to keep blowing away, in meditation and then during the day, especially in your relationships. This world is a blacksmith's shop, with fires all around, where we return good will for ill will and love for hatred, work harmoniously with others, and put other people's welfare before our own. All these are for putting out the fire of selfishness, which brings a deep sense of wellness to body and mind alike.

To have perfect detachment, the Gita says, we have to rise above not only "I and mine," but also pleasure and pain. This is precise, universal advice. Whether you live in America or in Asia, in a palace or in a hovel, you cannot escape the duality of pleasure and pain that is woven into the very fabric of life. A permanent state of security can never come to any person who is dependent upon external circumstances and satisfactions, for these all have a definite beginning and a finite end. No lasting joy, no lasting security can be ours if we pursue finite things, things that pass away.

But it takes a long time for most of us to learn that pleasure is not permanent. Most people get frustrated because unconsciously this is what all of us are trying to do: isolate ourselves in a pain-free world. That is the desire behind a great many technological advances, particularly where drugs are concerned. I am not opposed to painkillers in the hands of a wise physician, but I know too that whatever we do, pain is an integral part of life.

Hostility, too, is an unavoidable part of life. Even if you have ninety-nine persons cheering you, there will always be a hundredth to slander you. That is the nature of life, and to deal with it, we have to learn not to be always on the outlook for appreciation and applause. If people say, "Oh, there is nobody like you," don't get elated. Don't pick up your telephone and call your friends and tell them all the nice things that are being said about you. That's why so many people sink into depression when fortune seems to frown. During reversals of fortune, which will come to all of us, we can maintain our equanimity and tranquility. We do not need any external support because we are complete in ourselves.

＊

In our ancient Hindu tradition, we say that within every human being there are two forces deep in consciousness. One is the force of infatuation: selfish attachments, delusion, compulsion, hostility, violence. It is from these that the death-force draws its power. There is infatuation for money, infatuation for pleasure, infatuation for prestige, and the worst, infatuation for power. Jesus warned us of this force when he said, "All they who take the sword shall perish by the sword." The violent force of selfishness drives us toward death, but when we renounce violence and hostility, we go beyond death in this very life.

The sages of both East and West say that detachment and selflessness are a second force, which takes us over death into eternal life. If you can renounce all that is selfish and petty, you will attain the supreme state in which you know you are neither your body nor your mind but the one Self, utterly beyond change and death.

In my ancestral family, at least when I was growing up, people who were approaching the evening of life made preparations for the great journey. This is the glory of Buddhism and Hinduism: people know that the boat is coming, and they know that they have to put their house in order and prepare to leave all their luggage behind. When the time comes, they are prepared. And then a quite extraordinary thing happens: for them Death is no longer a frightening ogre; Death is a doorman. When the time comes, he opens the door and says, "After you."

✳

From the unreal, lead me to the real
From darkness, lead me to light.
From death, lead me to immortality.

This sublime prayer for immortality has been repeated in India for thousands of years, and it is as meaningful today as it was millennia ago. Living for pleasure is living in an unreal world, a dark world. The satisfaction that wealth and pleasure can give is as transient as a dream. Living for others – for our family, our community, our country, the whole world – is living in light.

This body of mine is not me but the car I drive. I rent it here; I leave it there. I rent it for a selfless purpose, and after many decades, when it is no longer functioning well, I will leave it . . . quietly, with no fuss and no regrets.

"Once we attain that abiding joy beyond the senses," the Bhagavad Gita says, "there is nothing more to be desired. We can no longer be shaken even by the heaviest burden of sorrow." When you have received this gift, what more can the world give you? What temptations can the world hold?

Without Self-realization, every satisfaction, every pleasure, every reward will be taken from us sooner or later by death. This is not a morbid reflection. It enriches life, gives it meaning, keeps us aware that every moment is precious. The sooner we begin to wake ourselves up, the better, for there is far to go. But at any age, the best time is now, because Death is walking close beside us.

Any day death can claim any one of us. But if you can wake yourself up, as the Buddha did, you live in freedom everywhere, in this world and the next. Terms like heaven and hell become pointless. Wherever you go is home, and whatever you do will bear good fruit. It doesn't matter when or where. You lose all curiosity about where you are going in your next life. Wherever you go, your life will flower and bear fruit for all.

Just because this body is shed, my life is not at an end. I know that there is a presence inside, a divine resident who will endure. Even after I have shed my physical body, all the love in my heart – which is not physical, not limited by time and space – will continue, and I will come back in a new body to be reunited with those I have loved and who have loved me – over and over again. People who love deeply, who help greatly, will be together again. This realization removes all fear of death from our hearts and gives us not only courage but understanding in the face of death.

In the Buddhist ideal, the *bodhisattva* is one who takes a vow to be reborn again and again to help relieve the suffering of others. You have reached the end of sorrow, yet you are free to say, "That green earth I lived on has become polluted. I can't just stay here and bask in bliss; I have to go back and do whatever I can to help. War is still stalking the earth, and I don't want even one young person to suffer. Let me go back and help to bring people together in harmony."

Your next life is not dependent upon a throw of the dice. It is dependent entirely on you. As you live today, so will your life be tomorrow. No outsider dictates it. As you live in this life, so will your life be next time; no fate ordains it for you. Instead of being afraid of death and what comes after, you can almost look forward to it just as you look forward to a new day, by preparing for your next life here and now. This is the joy of the Buddha's message: take your life in your hands, learn to practice meditation, change selfish modes of thinking into selfless, make your mind secure where it is insecure, extend your love to embrace all life, and then give and give and give.

✳

The Buddha would look at the roses in a garden and say, "They are so beautiful today, but by tonight they will have withered on their stem." Yet next year in the garden there will not be a desert, but roses again.

Every step of evolution involves a death. In an inspired poem, the Sufi mystic Jalaluddin Rumi lays out the long travail of our climb up the evolutionary scale. Death, he says, has never made us any less, but always more. To evolve into our full humanity, it is necessary to shake off the urges and appetites of the animal and die to all that makes us selfish, violent, and separate. Yet in Rumi's eyes, even the highest human level is not the end. For it is our fate one day to be united with the Infinite.

> I died as mineral and became a plant,
> I died as plant and rose to animal,
> I died as animal and I was Man.
> Why should I fear? When was I less by dying?
> Yet once more I shall die as Man, to soar
> With angels blest; but even from angelhood
> I must pass on: all except God doth perish.

When I have sacrificed my angel-soul,
I shall become what no mind e'er conceived.
Oh, let me not exist! for Non-existence
Proclaims in organ tones, "To Him we shall
    return."

An Eight-Point Program

The method of meditation I teach is universal. It can be practiced within the mainstream of any religious tradition, and outside all of them as well. When I began teaching meditation, I simply taught what I myself had been practicing for over a decade, illustrating from the scriptures and mystics of the world's great religions. Gradually this became systematized into eight points, the first and most important of which is meditation. The next few pages are a short introduction to this Eight-Point Program for spiritual growth. If you would like a more detailed presentation, all these points are discussed more fully in my book *Meditation*.

I. MEDITATION

The heart of this program is meditation: half an hour every morning, as early as is convenient.

Do not increase this period; if you want to meditate more, have half an hour in the evening also, preferably at the very end of the day.

Set aside a room in your home to be used only for meditation and spiritual reading. After a while that room will become associated with meditation in your mind, so that simply entering it will have a calming effect. If you cannot spare a room, have a particular corner. Whichever you choose, keep your meditation place clean, well ventilated, and reasonably austere.

Sit in a straight-backed chair or on the floor and gently close your eyes. If you sit on the floor, you may need to support your back lightly against a wall. You should be comfortable enough to forget your body, but not so comfortable that you become drowsy.

Whatever position you choose, be sure to keep your head, neck, and spinal column erect in a straight line. As concentration deepens, the nervous system relaxes and you may begin to fall asleep. It is important to resist this tendency right from the beginning, by drawing yourself up and away from your back support until the wave of sleep has passed.

Once you have closed your eyes, begin to go slowly, in your mind, through one of the passages from the scriptures or the great mystics which I recommend for use in meditation. I usually suggest learning first the Prayer of Saint Francis of Assisi:

Lord, make me an instrument of thy peace.
Where there is hatred, let me sow love;
Where there is injury, pardon;
Where there is doubt, faith;
Where there is despair, hope;
Where there is darkness, light;
Where there is sadness, joy.

O divine Master, grant that I may not so much
    seek
To be consoled as to console,
To be understood as to understand,
To be loved as to love;
For it is in giving that we receive;
It is in pardoning that we are pardoned;
It is in dying to self that we are born to eternal
    life.

When memorizing the prayer, it may be helpful to remind yourself that you are not addressing some extraterrestrial being outside.

The kingdom of heaven is within us, and the Lord is enshrined in the depths of our own consciousness. In this prayer we are calling deep into ourselves, appealing to the spark of the divine that is our real nature.

While you are meditating, do not follow any association of ideas or try to think about the passage. If you are giving your attention to each word, the meaning cannot help sinking in. When distractions come, do not resist them, but give more attention to the words of the passage. If your mind strays from the passage entirely, bring it back gently to the beginning and start again. When you reach the end of the passage, you may use it again as necessary to complete your period of meditation until you have memorized others.

It is helpful to have a wide variety of passages for meditation, drawn from the world's major traditions. Each passage should be positive and practical, drawn from a major scripture or from a mystic of the highest stature. I especially recommend the following:

The Twenty-third Psalm
The Shema

The Lord's Prayer
The Beatitudes
Saint Paul's "Epistle on Love"
    (1 Corinthians 13)
Thomas a Kempis, *Imitation of Christ* III.5
    ("The Wonderful Effect of Divine Love")
The Dhammapada, Chapters 1 and 26
Selections from the Bhagavad Gita:
    2.54–72 ("The Illumined Man")
    9.26–34 ("Make It an Offering")
    12.1–20 ("The Way of Love")
    18.49–73 ("Be Aware of Me Always")
Ansari of Herat, "Invocations"

These passages, along with many others equally beautiful selected from the world's religions, can be found in my collection *God Makes the Rivers to Flow* (Nilgiri Press, 1994).

The secret of meditation is simple: we become what we meditate on. When you use the Prayer of Saint Francis every day in meditation, you are driving the words deep into your consciousness. Eventually they become an integral part of your personality, which means they will find constant expression in what you do, what you say, and what you think.

2. REPETITION OF THE MANTRAM

A mantram, a Holy Name, is a powerful spiritual formula which has the capacity to transform consciousness when it is repeated silently in the mind. There is nothing magical about this. It is simply a matter of practice, as you can verify for yourself.

Every religious tradition has a mantram, often more than one. For Christians, the name of Jesus itself is a powerful mantram. Catholics also use *Hail Mary* or *Ave Maria.* Jews may use *Barukh attah Adonai,* "Blessed art thou, O Lord," or the Hasidic formula *Ribono shel olam,* "Lord of the universe." Muslims repeat the name of Allah or *Allahu akbar,* "God is great." Probably the oldest Buddhist mantram is *Om mani padme hum,* referring to the "jewel in the lotus" of the heart. In Hinduism, among many choices, I recommend *Rama, Rama,* which was Mahatma Gandhi's mantram, or the longer mantram I received from my own spiritual teacher, my grandmother:

Haré Rama Haré Rama,
Rama Rama Haré Haré,
Haré Krishna Haré Krishna,
Krishna Krishna Haré Haré.

Select a mantram that appeals to you deeply. In many traditions it is customary to take the mantram used by your spiritual teacher. Then, once you have chosen, do not change your mantram. Otherwise you will be like a person digging shallow wells in many places; you will never go deep enough to find water.

Repeat your mantram silently whenever you get the chance: while walking, while waiting, while you are doing mechanical chores like washing dishes, and especially when you are falling asleep. You will find for yourself that this is not mindless repetition. The mantram will help to keep you relaxed and alert during the day, and when you can fall asleep in it, it will go on working for you throughout the night as well.

Whenever you are angry or afraid, nervous or worried or resentful, repeat the mantram until the agitation subsides. The mantram works to steady the mind, and all these emotions are power running against you which the mantram can harness and put to work.

3. SLOWING DOWN

Hurry makes for tension, insecurity, inefficiency, and superficial living, even illness. Among other things, "hurry sickness" is a major component of the Type A behavior pattern which research has linked to heart disease. To guard against hurrying through the day, start the day early and simplify your life so that you do not try to fill your time with more than you can do. When you find yourself beginning to speed up, repeat your mantram to help you slow down.

It is important here not to confuse slowness with sloth or carelessness. In slowing down we should attend meticulously to details, giving our very best even to the smallest undertaking.

4. ONE-POINTED ATTENTION

Doing more than one thing at a time divides attention and fragments consciousness. When we read and eat at the same time, for example, part of our mind is on what we are reading and part on what we are eating; we are not getting the most from either activity. Similarly, when talking with someone, give him or her your full attention. These are little things, but together they help to unify consciousness and deepen concentration.

Everything we do should be worthy of our full attention. When the mind is one-pointed it will be secure, free from tension, and capable of the concentration that is the mark of genius in any field

5. TRAINING THE SENSES

In the food we eat, the books and magazines we read, the movies we see, all of us are subject to the conditioning of rigid likes and dislikes. To free ourselves from this conditioning, we need to learn to change our likes and dislikes freely when it is in the best interests of those around us or ourselves. We should choose to eat what our body needs, for example, rather than what the taste buds demand.

Similarly, the mind eats too, through the senses. In this age of mass media, we need to be particularly discriminating in what we read and what we go to see for entertainment, for we become in part what our senses take in.

6. PUTTING OTHERS FIRST

Dwelling on ourselves builds a wall between ourselves and others. Those who keep thinking about *their* needs, *their* wants, *their* plans, *their* ideas cannot help becoming lonely and insecure. The simple but effective technique I recommend is to learn to put other people first – beginning within the circle of your family and friends, where there is already a basis of love on which to build. When two people try to put each other first, for example, they are not only moving closer to each other. They are also removing the barriers of their ego-prison, which deepens their relationships with everyone else as well.

7. READING IN MYSTICISM

We are so surrounded today by a low concept of what the human being is that it is essential to give ourselves a higher image. For this reason I recommend devoting half an hour or so each day to reading the scriptures and the writings of the great mystics of all religions. Just before bedtime, after evening meditation, is a particularly good time, because the thoughts you fall asleep in will be with you throughout the night.

There is a helpful distinction between works of inspiration and works of spiritual instruction. Inspiration may be drawn from every tradition or religion. Instructions in meditation and other spiritual disciplines, however, can differ from and even seem to contradict each other. For this reason, it is wise to confine instructional reading to the works of one teacher or path. Choose your teacher carefully. A good teacher lives what he or she teaches, and it is the student's responsibility to exercise sound judgment. Then, once you have chosen, give your teacher your full loyalty.

8. SPIRITUAL ASSOCIATION

When we are trying to change our life, we need the support of others with the same goal. If you have friends who are meditating along the lines suggested here, it is a great help to meditate together regularly. Share your times of entertainment too; relaxation is an important part of spiritual living.

✳

This eightfold program, if it is followed sincerely and systematically, begins to transform personality almost immediately, leading to profoundly beneficial changes which spread to those around us.

Further Reading

Other works by Eknath Easwaran develop the themes in this book:

Dialogue with Death explores in greater depth the lesson death has to teach us about how to live. It takes its inspiration from the Katha Upanishad, which begins with the story of a teenager who goes to the King of Death himself to learn what happens when we die. The teachings given in reply are practical, lyrical, and profound.

The Bhagavad Gita for Daily Living is a verse-by-verse commentary on India's best-known scripture, which consistently throws light on the central questions of life and death. The three volumes in this set embrace the whole of Easwaran's teaching.

Easwaran's translations of India's scriptures are also available as single volumes in the Classics of Indian Spirituality series: *The Bhagavad Gita, The Upanishads*, and *The Dhammapada*.

Meditation is a step-by-step guide to the practice of meditation and the other steps in Easwaran's Eight-Point Program. A companion volume, *The Unstruck Bell,* is devoted to use of the mantram or Holy Name; one chapter is devoted to its use at the time of death.

Cassette tapes by Easwaran include:

Meditation, a series of warm talks in which Easwaran gives instructions in his Eight-Point Program to a live audience

Sacred Literature of the World, readings from inspiring passages for meditation from the world's religions, selected from Easwaran's anthology *God Makes the Rivers to Flow*

Index